AROUND THE WORLD

WITH THE WORD FRIENDS

Anne Civardi

Illustrated by Graham Philpot

Millie Mouse

Gertie Giraffe

Ellie Elephant

Molly Monkey and baby

Sam Squirrel

Bill Bird

Freddie Frog

Kelly Kangaroo

Old Croc

and me

Boris Bear

Hilda Hippo

Patsy Pig

Leo Lion

Ollie Octopus

Dudley Dog

Roger Rabbit

Derek Duck

Carly Cat

Willie Worm

These are the **Word Friends.**

THIS BOOK BELONGS TO

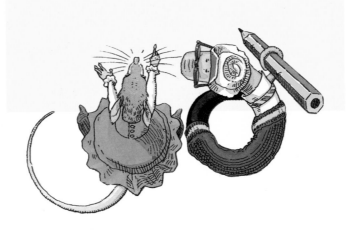

Contents

Getting ready to go

On a beautiful bright sunny morning, with the wind blowing gently, the Word Friends got ready to go on a long, exciting journey in their big yellow balloon. They were off to see all their animal friends who lived in lots of different countries around the world.

Old Croc was in charge of loading the balloon with all the things the Friends needed on their trip. He made sure that none of them took too much luggage.

Ollie Octopus was the navigator. He had worked out the route they were going to take, and he made sure that the big balloon flew in the right direction. Before they left, he showed the Friends which places they were going to visit on a big map of the world. Some of them were very hot and dry places, others were very wet. But their first stop was going to be in a very cold place.

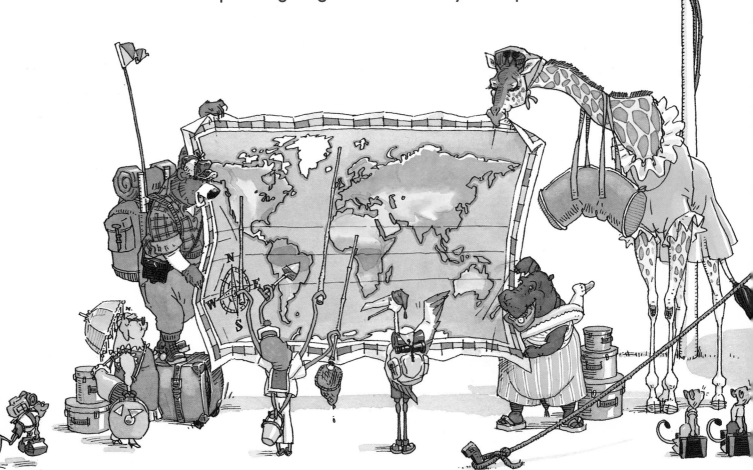

A Very Cold Place

On the trip around the world, Boris Bear visited his old friend, the polar bear, who lives in the Arctic, a very cold place, with lots of other animals.

The Eskimos, or Inuits, live here too. The sea freezes over in winter and the land is covered in snow nearly all year round.

Eskimo house

fish drying

Eskimo fishing

Welcome Boris

Arctic tern

Eskimos (Inuits)

huskies

snowmobile

Boris Bear

sled

A Very Hot Place

hawk

adobe houses

thorn bush

water hole

date palm

oasis

fennec fox

ostrich

camel

Jack rabbits

For three days, the Word Friends traveled across the desert, riding on big, strong camels.

Only a few types of animals and plants can live in the desert, because it is so hot, dry and sandy.

desert rats

8

antelopes

sand dune

acacia tree

nomads' belongings

goat

mule

nomads

well

scorpion

lizard

cobra

In the middle of the desert, the Friends came across a family of nomads living in a tent.

Nomads move from place to place and set up camp near a well.

9

In the Country

One day, the Word Friends decided to go camping in the woods. Boris Bear was their leader.

They walked through fields and meadows, picked flowers and watched the animals, insects, and birds.

Bill Bird went birdwatching.

Roger Rabbit helped to dig a burrow.

While Willie Worm fished in a pond, Derek Duck rode on the back of a big swan. Millie Mouse talked to her friends, the field mice.

That night, the Friends pitched their tents deep in the woods. They sang songs and cooked delicious food around the camp fire.

Around the campsite, some animals, who were out hunting for food, watched the happy Friends. How many can you see?

11

A Very Wet Place

Speeding through a grassy swamp in an airboat, the Friends saw many birds. In hot, wet places, there are lots of worms and insects for birds to eat.

Old Croc watched baby alligators hatch. Ollie Octopus fed the big turtles who were swimming in the water.

sawgrass

racoons

cormorants

seacow

snakebirds

moccasin snake

crocodiles

coon oysters

fiddler crabs

alligators

baby alligators

alligator nest

On the Plains

vultures

weaver birds

baboons

tribesmen

lion

leopard

hyenas

oxpecker bird

lioness

water buffalo

rhinocerus

14   lion cubs

On safari, the Friends had an exciting time driving across the hot, grassy plains in their jeeps. Boris Bear took photographs of a big rhino, some funny baboons and a sleepy leopard who was lying in a tree.

Kelly Kangaroo nearly bumped into a herd of stampeding zebras when they galloped in front of her jeep. Ellie Elephant had fun playing with some wild elephants who were drinking at a water hole.

impalas

elephants

giraffe

crocodiles

hippopotamus

cheetahs

ostriches

zebras

wildebeest

In the Mountains

High up in the rocky mountains, Boris Bear talked to a huge grizzly bear, and Leo Lion met a fierce puma who lived on the steep mountainside.

Only a few animals live in such a high place because it is so cold and windy, and it is hard to find food. They have thick fur to keep them warm.

Nearby, Ellie Elephant and Gertie Giraffe raced down a snowy mountain on their fast skis.

eagle

wolves

bighorn sheep

mountain goats

puma

grizzly bear

porcupine

snowshoe hare

bear cub

skunks

hang-glider

cable car

chipmunks

chairlift

skiers

moose

ground hogs

beavers

In the Jungle

hummingbird

howler monkeys

gibbon

spider monkeys

spider

jaguar

anaconda snake

alligator

capybaras

Paddling slowly through the hot, humid jungle, the Word Friends were surrounded by all kinds of animals, insects, and birds.

Some of them lived high up in the treetops where there was plenty of sunlight, and lots of leaves, flowers, and fruits to feed on.

toucan

parrot

sloth

tree porcupine

chameleon

gorillas

tree boa snake

armadillo

electric eel

tree frog

anteater

iguana   ant hill

Others, like the giant anteater, armadillo, and capybara lived under the trees, where it was dark and gloomy and rained nearly every day.

Molly Monkey met two chatty spider monkeys hanging from a big branch, and Leo Lion saw his friend, the jaguar, climbing up a tall tree.

In the City

One afternoon, the Friends flew into a big, busy city where lots of people lived and worked. While they were there, they stayed in a big hotel and visited a famous museum.

skyscraper

office building

car park

church

shops

hospital

bank

post office

police station

hotel

school

fire station

department store

museum

garage

Leo Lion had his mane cut at the barber's shop.

Ollie Octopus and Freddie Frog went shopping for toys.

Every morning, Old Croc bought the newspaper to read.

Roger Rabbit raced Millie Mouse through the busy streets.

One evening, Boris Bear took Patsy Pig to a café for dinner.

Molly Monkey bought a big bag of ripe bananas.

At the Beach

Molly Monkey waterskiing

Old Croc surfing

Hilda Hippo swimming

buoy

sail boat

windsurfer

surfboard

flippers

umbrella

mattress

starfish

sea anemones

crab

sea urchin

fish

hermit crab

shrimp

mussels

seaweed

The tired Friends decided to stop traveling for a while to have a restful vacation at the beach.

They had a wonderful time playing on the sand, swimming in the blue sea, surfing, water-skiing, and sunbathing.

lighthouse

cliff

motorboat

seagull

lifeguards

lounge chair

bucket and shovel

sandcastle

worm

ice cream

shells

life raft

Derek Duck's catch!

Kelly Kangaroo windsurfing

Patsy Pig sunbathing

Every day, Ollie Octopus sat by the side of a rockpool and talked to the crabs, starfish, and sea anemones.

Bill Bird and Freddie Frog were the lifeguards. They made sure that everyone was safe in the sea.

In the Outback

dingo

dingo
pup

emu

emu chick

lyrebird

kangaroo

stick insect

frilled
lizard

wallaby

joey

rabbit

Kelly Kangaroo's favorite place
to visit was the hot, dry outback
where she met lots of other animals
who keep their babies in pouches.

Molly Monkey had never seen so
many strange creatures or so many
colorful birds singing in the trees.

24

cockatoos

possum

kookaburras

gum tree

koala bears

parakeets

Aborigines

eucalyptus tree

zebra finches

mulga snake

wombat

echidna

thorny devil

duck-billed platypus

Old Croc enjoyed talking to some Aborigines as they walked through the outback hunting for food.

Aborigines are nomads who are very good at finding their way and living in the bush and in the desert.

In the Harbor

One morning at the crack of dawn, the Word Friends went to the harbor.

They helped the fisherman, Captain Salt, get his fishing boat ready.

Far out at sea, Captain Salt put the fishing net into the cold water.

When the net was full of wriggling fish, Ollie helped him haul it in.

At the end of a hard day's work, the fishermen sailed back to the harbor.

They unloaded the boxes of fish and washed down the fishing boat.

Later on, Ollie helped Captain Salt sell his big catch on the dock.

Patsy Pig bought three fresh fish to give to Boris Bear for dinner.

At the Carnival

For four happy days and nights, the Word Friends had a wonderful time at a big carnival.

Wearing magnificent costumes and headdresses, they made lots of noise as they danced and sang in the streets.

fireworks

dragon

flag

acrobats

strongman

balloons

clown

tambourine

hoop

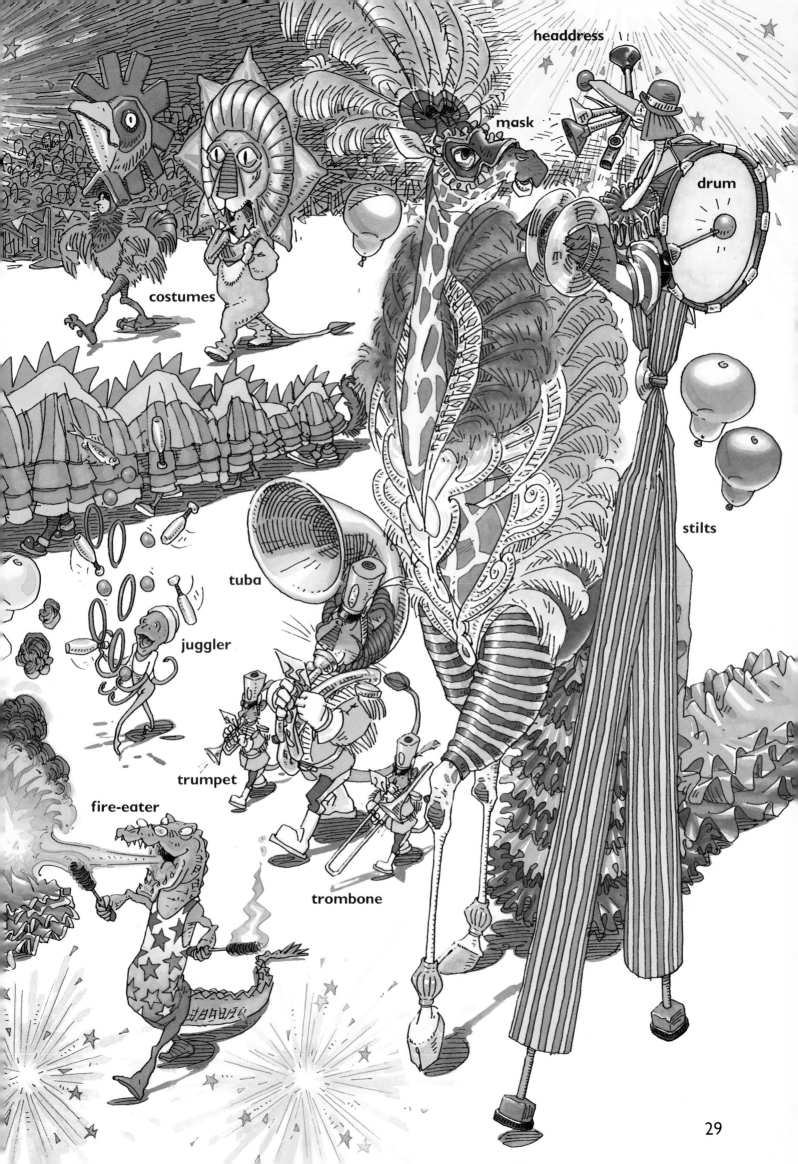

headdress

mask

drum

costumes

stilts

tuba

juggler

trumpet

trombone

fire-eater

29

Under the Sea

Deep under the sea, Ollie Octopus said hello to an old friend, and he met lots of other strange-looking sea creatures.

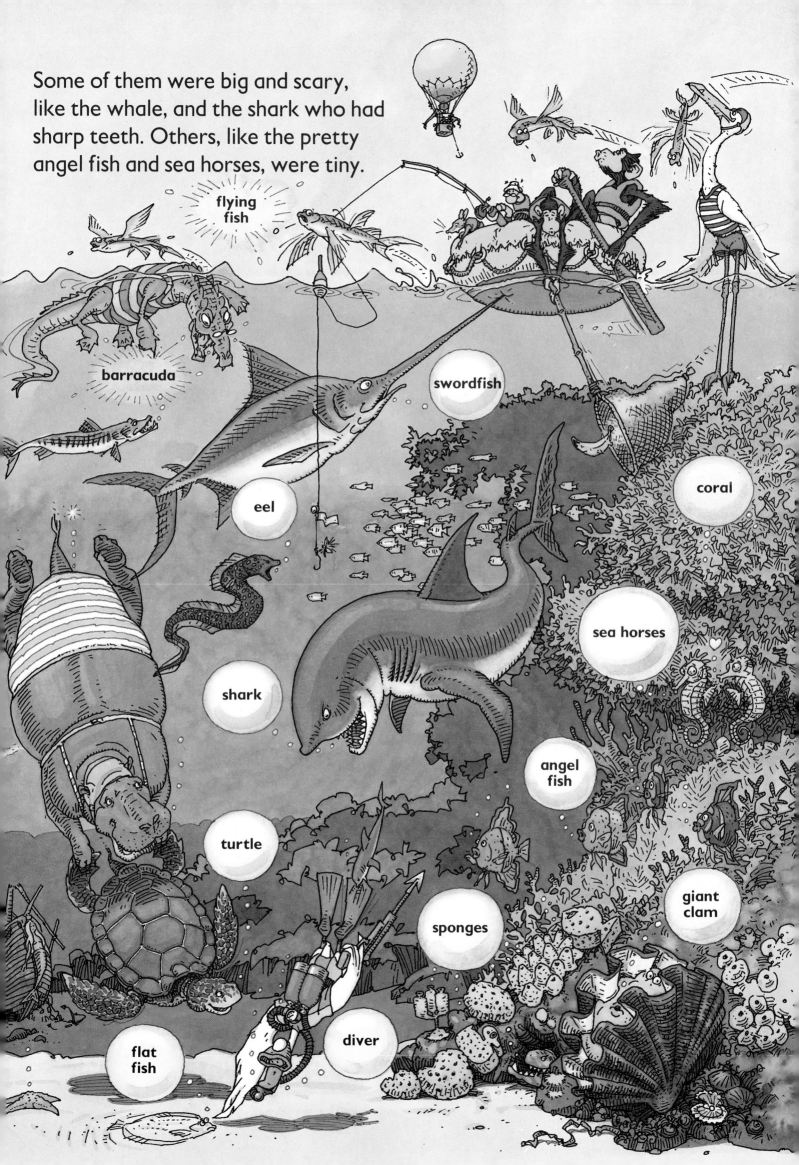

Some of them were big and scary, like the whale, and the shark who had sharp teeth. Others, like the pretty angel fish and sea horses, were tiny.

flying fish

barracuda

swordfish

coral

eel

sea horses

shark

angel fish

turtle

giant clam

sponges

flat fish

diver

On a Farm

field

cows

corn field

hay bales

tractor

farmer

milking barn

bull

farm truck

pigs

piglets

horse

pigpen

Early one morning, the Word Friends landed their balloon in a big field on a farm. They had fun helping the farmer with his work.

Dudley Dog helped the sheepdog to round up the sheep. Ellie Elephant helped the farmer's wife load heavy bales of hay on to the tractor.

orchard

sheep

shepherd

lambs

sheepdog

silo

farmhouse

rabbits

barn

barn owl

farm owner

neighbor

hen house

farm cat

rat

goat

geese

care-taker

ducks

chickens

Bill Bird helped to collect the chickens' eggs from the hen house. Later they were sorted by sizes and taken to market.

When it was time for the cows to be milked in the milking barn, Ollie Octopus tried to milk two of the cows himself.

Traveling

Sometimes, instead of flying around in their big yellow balloon, the Friends used other kinds of transportation to travel from place to place. Here are some of them.

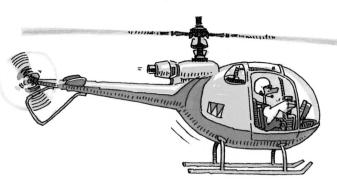

Derek Duck's favorite way to travel was by **helicopter**.

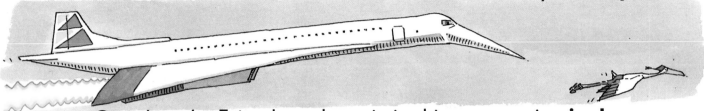

One day, the Friends took a trip in this supersonic **airplane**. Bill Bird thought that it looked just like him.

Molly Monkey drove around the city on a yellow **motorcycle**.

Leo Lion took his cubs for a ride in a snazzy **sports car**.

Hilda Hippo was a bit too heavy for this **rickshaw**.

Boris Bear sang to Patsy Pig as he paddled down a canal in a **gondola**.

The Friends went to the beach in this sleek new **bus**.

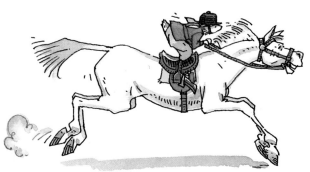

Roger Rabbit galloped across the countryside on a white **horse**.

On the farm, Willie and Millie rode in a **donkey-drawn cart**.

Patsy Pig had a lovely lazy day with Boris Bear traveling down a river on a colorful **barge**.

Gertie Giraffe sailed to a hot place on a **sailing ship**.

Leo Lion took his sports car when he traveled by **ferry**.

All the Word Friends caught this express **train** to the mountains.

Favorite Food

Most of the food they ate on their trip was quite different from the kind that the Word Friends were used to at home.

Leo Lion liked the meat dishes, but Molly Monkey and Patsy Pig preferred the exotic fruits, and vegetables.

hamburger and french fries

meatballs

soda drink

milkshake

shish kebab

coffee

fruit salad

tortilla

caviar

tea

nut bread

fried rice

pickled herring

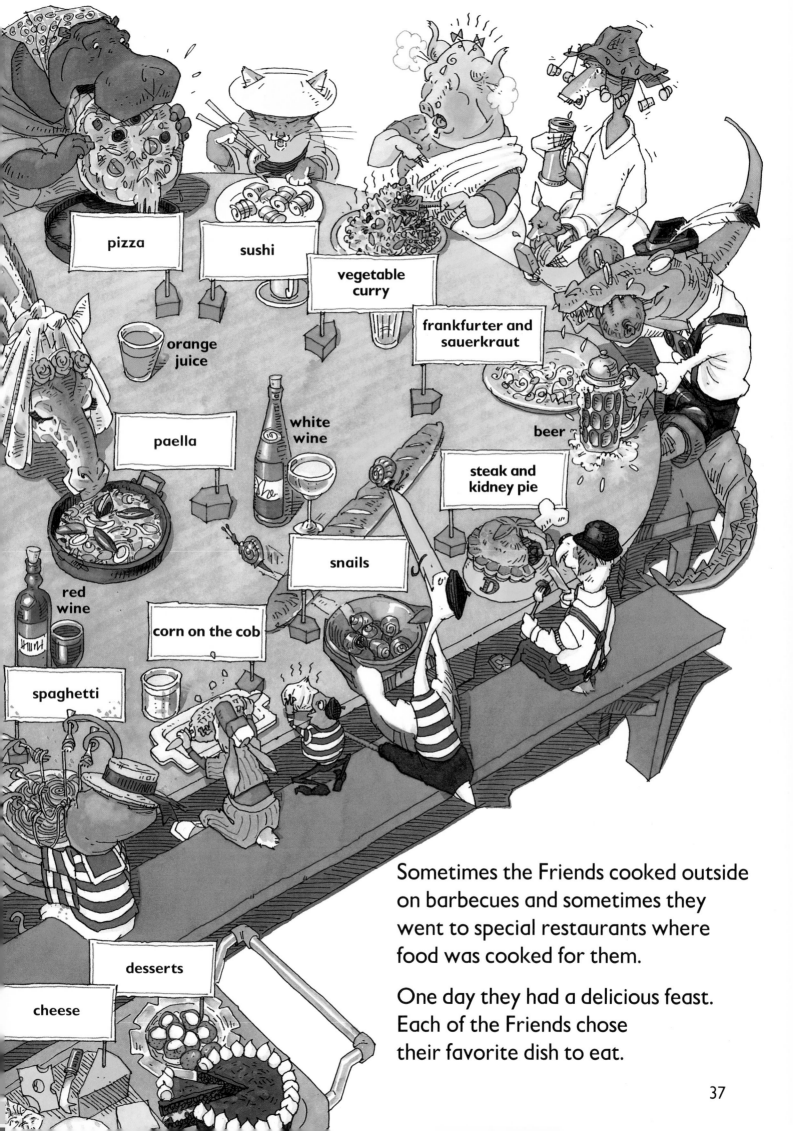

pizza

sushi

vegetable
curry

orange
juice

frankfurter and
sauerkraut

paella

white
wine

beer

steak and
kidney pie

snails

red
wine

corn on the cob

spaghetti

desserts

cheese

Sometimes the Friends cooked outside on barbecues and sometimes they went to special restaurants where food was cooked for them.

One day they had a delicious feast. Each of the Friends chose their favorite dish to eat.

Homes

This strange **hut** was made of branches covered with cow dung.

These people lived in the hot desert in a tent called a **yurt**.

A small family lived in this **trailer** on a special campsite.

Built around a courtyard, this **farmhouse** was made of mud bricks.

The people in this **houseboat** rowed to land for their shopping.

This **reed house** was built in the middle of a swampy marsh.

All over the world, people live in different kinds of homes. Some live in boats or trailers, others in houses built of bricks, wood, mud or reeds.

When they got home, Ollie, Millie and Freddie painted a mural of some of the houses they had stayed in for all their friends to see.

This **longhouse** was built on stilts close to a big river.

This block of **apartments** was built in the middle of a busy city.

Carved out of soft rock, these **cave houses** looked very odd.

The snow on this wooden **chalet** kept it very warm.

This lovely big **house** was built outside a crowded city.

Growing Things

Wherever they went, the Friends worked hard in the fields, orchards and plantations, helping the busy farmers to harvest their crops.

On hot sunny days, they filled big baskets with ripe grapes, oranges, pineapples and bananas to be sent abroad or sold at market.

Hilda Hippo sang songs as she picked **tea leaves** off the plants.

Ollie Octopus planted rows and rows of **rice** in a wet paddy field.

The big bunches of **bananas** that Molly cut down were very heavy.

Kelly Kangaroo had to jump up high to pick the **oranges**.

Only Gertie Giraffe could reach the highest **coconuts**.

40

Patsy Pig hid from Boris Bear in a big field of **sunflowers**.

Bill Bird tasted the sweet **grapes** he picked off the vines.

Sam Squirrel cut down the big **cocoa pods** growing on this tree.

Cutting down **sugar cane** was hard and hot work for Leo Lion.

Old Croc found it a prickly job collecting **pineapples**.

Millie Mouse watched a combine harvester cut down ripe **wheat**.

Boris and Leo sawed down a very tall tree to be used for **timber**.

Sports to play

All over the world, the Word Friends learned how to play games that they had never played before. These are some of their favorite ones.

Basketball

Gertie was the best basketball player because she was so tall.

Ice Hockey

Derek Duck found it very difficult to shoot the puck past Boris Bear.

Tennis

Even with five rackets, Ollie Octopus couldn't beat Patsy Pig at tennis.

Baseball

Roger Rabbit hit five home runs in a baseball game.

Cricket

wicket keeper · batsman · fielder · bowler · umpire

Molly Monkey bowled out Bill Bird when the Friends played cricket.

Rugby

Leo Lion was tackled by Kelly Kangaroo but still scored two goals.

goalposts

American Football

helmet · shoulder pad · cheerleaders

Patsy Pig cheered on her football team from the sidelines.

Ping Pong

net · bat

Willie Worm taught Millie Mouse how to play ping pong.

Soccer

goalie · referee

Roger Rabbit was so good at soccer that he scored six goals.

Famous Places

While she was away, Molly Monkey collected postcards of all the famous buildings she saw. As soon as she got home, she stuck her favorite ones on a bulletin board to remind her of the amazing places she had visited.

AMERICA

Statue of Liberty

FRANCE

Eiffel Tower

Tower of London – ENGLAND

Taj Mahal – INDIA

Parthenon – GREECE

At the end of their incredible trip, the Word Friends put all their photographs into an album.

These are just a few of them. Can you remember where they took each of these wonderful pictures?

Designed by
Graham Philpot
and
Alison Fenton

Consultant: Michael Boorer

First Published in 1989
Conran Octopus Limited
37 Shelton Street, London WC2H 9HN

This edition published by
Derrydale Books
distributed by Crown Publishers Inc.,
225 Park Avenue South,
New York, New York 10003

ISBN 0-517-69407-7

hgfedcba

Typeset by Capital Setters, London.
Printed and bound in Italy.